T0055962

RALPH VAUGHAN WILLIAMS

SERENADE TO MUSIC

Words by Shakespeare

Vocal Score

MUSIC DEPARTMENT

OXFORD
UNIVERSITY PRESS

OXFORD
UNIVERSITY PRESS

Great Clarendon Street, Oxford OX2 6DP, England
198 Madison Avenue, New York, NY 10016, USA

Oxford University Press is a department of the University of Oxford.
It furthers the University's aim of excellence in research, scholarship,
and education by publishing worldwide in

Oxford New York
Auckland Bangkok Buenos Aires Cape Town Chennai
Dar es Salaam Delhi Hong Kong Istanbul Karachi Kolkata
Kuala Lumpur Madrid Melbourne Mexico City Mumbai Nairobi
São Paulo Shanghai Taipei Tokyo Toronto

Oxford is a registered trade mark of Oxford University Press
in the UK and in certain other countries

© Oxford University Press 1938. Renewed in USA 1966. This edition © Oxford University Press 2008.
This new edition prepared with the kind support of The Vaughan Williams Charitable Trust (formerly RVW Ltd.).

Ralph Vaughan Williams has asserted his right under the Copyright, Designs,
and Patents Act, 1988, to be identified as the Composer of this work

Database right Oxford University Press (maker)

All rights reserved. No part of this publication may be reproduced,
stored in a retrieval system, or transmitted, in any form or by any means,
without the prior permission in writing of Oxford University Press,
or as expressly permitted by law. Enquiries concerning reproduction
outside the scope of the above should be sent to the Music Copyright
Department, Oxford University Press, at the address above

Permission to perform this work in public (except in the course
of divine worship) should normally be obtained from the
Performing Right Society Ltd. (PRS), 29/33 Berners Street,
London W1P 4AA, or its affiliated Societies in each country
throughout the world, unless the owner or the occupier of
the premises being used holds a licence from the Society

Permission to make a recording must be obtained in advance
from the Mechanical-Copyright Protection Society Ltd. (MCPS),
Elgar House, 41 Streatham High Road, London SW16 1ER,
or its affiliated Societies in each country throughout the world

ISBN 978-0-19-336002-0

Engraved by Paul Broom.
Printed in Great Britain on acid-free paper by
Halstan & Co. Ltd., Amersham, Bucks.

INTRODUCTION

In January 1938 Vaughan Williams received a request from Sir Henry J. Wood for a work to be performed at a concert planned for 5 October 1938, to mark the fiftieth anniversary of his début as a conductor. Vaughan Williams replied that it would be an honour to compose something 'in your praise' and wondered if they should ask the Poet Laureate, John Masefield, for a text. Wood replied on 25 January that he did not want anything in praise of himself but rather 'a choral work that can be used at any time and for any occasion. I would not think of asking you to write a work that might only be used the once, which would naturally be the case were it written round myself.' Wood later suggested a work for sixteen singers who had sung many times with him at festivals and the Promenade Concerts. Vaughan Williams reported this to his friend Ursula Wood (who in 1953 was to become his second wife), adding that he had always wanted to set the Jessica and Lorenzo scene (Act V, Scene 1) from Shakespeare's *The Merchant of Venice*. 'Eight Jessicas and eight Lorenzos?' she asked. 'No, just a little bit for each voice.' Vaughan Williams sent Wood the manuscript of the work on 2 June. The sixteen singers were:

Sopranos	**Altos**	**Tenors**	**Basses**
Isobel Baillie	Margaret Balfour	Parry Jones	Norman Allin
Stiles Allen	Muriel Brunskill	Heddle Nash	Robert Easton
Elsie Suddaby	Astra Desmond	Frank Titterton	Roy Henderson
Eva Turner	Mary Jarred	Walter Widdop	Harold Williams

The parts allotted to each of these singers are indicated in the score by their initials, including their participation in choral passages. It is uncanny how Vaughan Williams captured the vocal characteristics of all sixteen in such brief phrases and we are fortunate that their artistry is preserved in the recording made a few days after the first performance. Who that heard them could fail to recognise Heddle Nash in 'Look how the floor of heaven is thick inlaid with patines of bright gold'? Or Eva Turner at 'How many things by season season'd are to their right praise and true perfection'? Or Isobel Baillie's ethereal 'Of sweet harmony' with which the work ends? Yet the marvel is that when later singers perform these passages they seem by alchemy to absorb the spirit of the originals while retaining their own individuality.

The *Serenade* can be performed by four solo singers (soprano, alto, tenor, and bass) and chorus or all the solo parts may be sung in chorus. There is also a version for orchestra without voices, made at Wood's suggestion in 1939. As Wood hoped, the *Serenade* has outlived the occasion for which it was written and is widely regarded as one of the most beautiful and inspired of all settings of Shakespeare.

Michael Kennedy
2008

SERENADE TO MUSIC

How sweet the moonlight sleeps upon this bank!
Here will we sit and let the sounds of music
Creep in our ears: soft stillness and the night
Become the touches of sweet harmony.
. . . Look how the floor of heaven
Is thick inlaid with patines of bright gold:
There's not the smallest orb that thou behold'st
But in his motion like an angel sings,
Still quiring to the young-ey'd cherubins;
Such harmony is in immortal souls;
But, whilst the muddy vesture of decay
Doth grossly close it in, we cannot hear it.
Come, ho! and wake Diana with a hymn:
With sweetest touches pierce your mistress' ear,
And draw her home with music.
I am never merry when I hear sweet music.
The reason is, your spirits are attentive:
. . . The man that hath no music in himself,
Nor is not mov'd with concord of sweet sounds,
Is fit for treasons, stratagems and spoils;
The motions of his spirit are as dull as night,
And his affections dark as Erebus;
Let no such man be trusted.
Music! Hark! . . . It is the music of the house.
Methinks it sounds much sweeter than by day.
Silence bestows that virtue on it . . .
How many things by season season'd are
To their right praise and true perfection!
Peace, ho! The moon sleeps with Endymion,
And would not be awak'd!
. . . Soft stillness and the night
Become the touches of sweet harmony.

(William Shakespeare, *c.*1564–1616, *The Merchant of Venice*)

Serenade to Music

William Shakespeare (*c.*1564–1616)

R. VAUGHAN WILLIAMS

Orchestral material is available on hire from the Publisher's Hire Library, or appropriate agent.

Printed in Great Britain

© Oxford University Press 1938. Renewed in USA 1966. New edition © Oxford University Press 2008.
This edition prepared with the kind support of The Vaugham Williams Charitable Trust (formerly RVW Ltd).

OXFORD UNIVERSITY PRESS, MUSIC DEPARTMENT, GREAT CLARENDON STREET, OXFORD, OX2 6DP
The Moral Rights of the Composer have been asserted. Photocopying this copyright material is ILLEGAL.

17
20
Poco animato
p
23
pp
B
26
29
poco rit.
tempo primo

32
TUTTI
S.A. I.B.
pp
E.S. E.T.
How sweet the moon - light sleeps up -
PRANO
M.Ba. A.D.
pp
M.Br. M.J.
How sweet the moon - light sleeps— up -
LTO
H.N. W.W.
pp
P.J. F.T.
How sweet the moon - light sleeps up -
ENOR
R.H. R.E.
pp
H.W. N.A.
How sweet the moon - light sleeps— up -
ASS
36
C
-on this bank! Here will we sit and let the
-on this bank! Here will we sit and let the
-on this bank! Here will we sit and let the
-on this bank! Here will we sit and let the
C

40
sounds of mu - sic Creep in our ears:
sounds of mu - sic Creep in our ears:
sounds of mu - sic Creep in our ears:
sounds of mu - sic Creep in our ears:
43
E.S. E.T.
I.B. S.A.
pp
Soft still - - - - - ness,
M.Br. M.J.
M.Ba. A.D.
pp
Soft still - - - - - ness,
P.J. F.T.
H.N. W.W.
pp
Soft still - - - -
H.W. N.A.
R.H. R.E.
pp
Soft still - - - -
pp

46
D
ppp
and the night,
ppp
and the night,
ppp
- ness, and the night,
ppp
- ness, and the night,
D
pp
49
I.B. E.S.
S.A. E.T.
Be - come the touch - - es of sweet
M.Ba. A.D.
M.Br. M.J.
Be - come the touch - - es of sweet
H.N. W.W.
P.J. F.T.
Be - come the touch - - es of sweet
R.E. R.H.
H.W. N.A.
Be - come the touch - - es of sweet

52
SOPRANO SOLO
I.B.
pp
har - - - - mo - ny,
of sweet
har - - - - mo - ny.
har - - - - mo - ny.
har - - - - mo - ny.
Vln Solo
56
E
S. SOLO
har - mo-ny.
61
Poco animato
pp

64
T. SOLO
H.N. p
Look how the floor of heaven Is thick in -
67
pp
- laid with pa - tines of bright
pp
69
F.T.
F
gold: There's not the small - est
pp
71
orb that thou be - holds't But in his mo - tion like an

74
W.W.
cresc.
an - - - gel sings, Still quir - ing to the young - ey'd
cresc.
77
che - - - - - - - - - - ru - bins;
79
G
TUTTI
S.A. E.T.
I.B. E.S.
Such har - - mo - ny
M.Ba M.Br.
A.D. M.J.
Such har - - mo - ny
H.N. W.W.
P.J. F.T.
Such har - - mo - ny
R.H. R.E.
H.W. N.A.
Such har - - mo - ny
S.
A.
T.
B.
G

81
is in im - mor - tal souls;
is in im - mor - tal souls;
is in im - mor - tal souls;
is in im - mor - tal souls;
84
T. SOLO
P.J. p
But whilst this mud - dy ves - - - ture
p
86
of de - cay Doth gross - ly close it in

89
H
TUTTI
unis. pp
S.
we can-not hear it.
unis. pp
A.
we can-not hear it.
unis. pp
T.
we can-not hear it.
unis. pp
B.
we can-not hear it.
H
pp
93
pp cresc.
97
K
S.A. f
S. SOLO
Come, ho! and wake Di-a-na with a hymn:
f
p
cresc.
p

101
With sweet-est touch-es pierce your mis-tress' ear,
fp
104
f
And draw her home with
cresc.
f
Tempo primo
107
L
S. SOLO
mu - - - - sic, with mu - - - sic.
TUTTI
E.T.
ff
S.
E.S. I.B.
And draw her home with mu - - - sic.
A.D. M.Ba.
ff
A.
M.Br. M.J.
And draw her home with mu - - - sic.
P.J. W.W.
ff
T.
H.N. F.T.
And draw her home with mu - - - sic.
R.E. R.H.
ff
B.
H.W. N.A.
And draw her home with mu - - - sic.
L
Tempo primo
ff

111
dim.
p
115
Andante con moto ♩ = 80
S. SOLO
SOPRANO SOLO E.S. p
I am nev - er mer - ry
pp
121
M
when I hear sweet mu - - - - - sic.
127
B. SOLO
BASS SOLO R.E. p
The rea - son is, your spi - rits are at - ten - tive:

131
H.W.
O
The man that hath no mu - sic in him -
137
R.H.
- self, Nor is not mov'd with con - cord of sweet
142
R.E.
sounds, Is fit for trea - sons,
146
stra - ta - gems and spoils;

150
P
N.A.
The mo - tions of his spi - rit are dull as night,
154
And his af - fec - tions dark as E - re - bus;
158
TUTTI
S.
unis. pp
Let no such man be trust - ed.
A.
unis. pp
Let no such man be trust - ed.
T.
unis. pp
Let no such man be trust - ed.
B.
unis. pp
Let no such man be trust - ed.

Q
Tempo primo (ma poco animato)
164
pp cresc.
167
M.Br. f
A. SOLO
Mu - sic! Hark!
f
p
poco rit.
171
Tempo primo
It is your mu - sic of the house.
f
p
174
A.D.
Me - thinks it sounds much sweet - er than by

177
R
M.J.
day.
Si - - - - - lence be -
180
- stows that vir - tue on it,
182
Poco animato
SOPRANO SOLO E.T.
p
S. SOLO
How ma - ny things by
p
184
sea - - son sea - son'd are
cresc.

186
f
To their right praise and
f
188
true per - fec - - - tion!
f
f
190
S
ALTO SOLO M.Ba. p
Peace, ho!
pp
192
pp
The moon sleeps

194
with En - dy - mi - on
And would not be a -
colla voce
196
poco rit.
- wak'd!
Vln Solo
a tempo
199
Tempo primo
T
TUTTI
I.B S.A.
ppp
E.S. E.T.
Soft still - -
S.
A.
T.
B.
H.N. F.T.
P.J. W.W.
R.E. R.H.
H.W. N.A.
Tempo primo
pp

202
- ness and the night
- ness and the night
- ness and the night
- ness and the night
205
Be - come the touch - - es of sweet
Be - come the touch - - es of sweet
Be - come the touch - - es of sweet
Be - come the touch - - es of sweet

Music engraved by Paul Broom.
Printed in England by Halstan & Co. Ltd., Amersham, Bucks.